THIS IS
A BOOK FOR
PEOPLE
WHO LOVE

CATS

THIS IS
A BOOK FOR
PEOPLE
WHO LOVE

CATS

ELIZA BERKOWITZ

ILLUSTRATED BY LUCY ROSE

RUNNING PRESS
PHILADELPHIA

Running Press
Hachette Book Group
1290 Avenue of the Americas, New York, NY 10104
www.runningpress.com
@Running_Press

Printed in China

First Edition: August 2023

Published by Running Press, an imprint of Perseus Books, LLC,
a subsidiary of Hachette Book Group, Inc. The Running Press
name and logo are trademarks of the Hachette Book Group.

The Hachette Speakers Bureau provides a wide range of authors for
speaking events. To find out more, go to www.hachettespeakersbureau.com
or email HachetteSpeakers@hbgusa.com.

Running Press books may be purchased in bulk for business,
educational, or promotional use. For more information, please
contact your local bookseller or the Hachette Book Group Special
Markets Department at Special.Markets@hbgusa.com.

The publisher is not responsible for websites (or their content)
that are not owned by the publisher.

Print book cover and interior design by Jenna McBride.

Library of Congress Control Number: 2022950462

ISBNs: 978-0-7624-8309-9 (hardcover), 978-0-7624-8311-2 (ebook)

APS

10 9 8 7 6 5 4 3 2 1

For Bunny, the shy, tiny fuzzball
who rescued me from a floof-free life.
And Lionel, the friendly, clever
cuddler who made every day
weird and fun. You both live on
forever in my heart.

CONTENTS

WHY WE LOVE CATS

If you have ever googled the phrase "Why do I like cats better than people?" you are not alone. While some prefer the company of humans, there are inevitable drawbacks to spending your time with them. People can be unreliable. They may have opinions you don't agree with. Many are also quick to offer unsolicited advice. Cats, on the other hand, are reliably adorable. They will never criticize you or be prone to chronic lateness. They will never borrow money and forget to pay you back. Cats can be counted on to act like cats—what a wonderful thing! The particulars of their personalities will vary from cat to cat, but we do have a general idea of the behaviors and traits you can expect. And although not all cat behaviors are ideal (those who have sacrificed  couches and curtains to tiny claws will understand), cats more than make up for it with their undeniably terrific qualities.

For cat lovers, a cuddle with a sweet feline is like a warm, sunny day after a week of rain. And there's a reason for this. When you pet a cat, your body releases a chemical called oxytocin. This is the hormone responsible for the rush of pleasant feelings you experience when you're falling in love. Petting a cat has also been shown to lower blood pressure and relieve stress. Cats can help sufferers of depression, anxiety, and PTSD by providing emotional support and companionship. It's no wonder that spending time with a feline friend can be so calming and restorative. And the pluses don't end there…Here are some other things we love about cats:

🐾 Their faces. Whether flat-faced with a scrunched-up nose or square-headed with big round eyes, every cat has a lovable little face. Their tiny noses are just begging to be booped.

🐾 Their fur. It's so soft! They usually like when you pet them, and if you're lucky you might even get to rest your face on them. (Hairless cats may not have fur, but their peach fuzz makes their skin soft like velvet!)

🐾 Their purr. Is there anything better than a warm ball of floof on your lap, purring away like a motor? No. There is not.

🐾 Their noises. From sweet *meows* to charming chattering, cats use sounds to communicate. Although we don't always understand what they're telling us, we love their delightful voices nonetheless.

🐾 Their weird personalities. Every cat has its own quirks and odd behaviors. Some cats are prone to staring at an invisible spot on the wall. Some will make a bed out of any bowl-shaped thing, even when there are comfier spots all over the house. Some get the zoomies every night for no conceivable reason. Cats are really weird!

🐾 Their stunning physical feats! Cats are experts at jumping and balancing, and their super coordination skills enable them to (almost) always land on their feet after a fall. They're so much fun to watch in action.

🐾 Their attention and affection. And since cats can be finicky about their people, it's incredibly gratifying to win one over. They make you work for it, but it's absolutely worth the effort.

Basically, cats are special creatures that make life better. Whether playing with a feather-on-a-string toy or curling up on the couch, you can be sure that quality time with a cat is time well spent. We can't resist their furry little faces and oddball behaviors!

WILD BEGINNINGS

With about 86 million in the United States, cats are the nation's most popular pet. It is estimated that 45.3 percent of households have at least one. And it's not only Americans who love their pet cats. In France, there are twice as many pet cats as pet dogs. In Europe, there are more than 110 million pet cats! Around the world, people are dedicated to their animals and will go to great lengths to care for and keep their kitties healthy. This hasn't always been the case, however; it's only in the last three hundred years or so that we have invited cats into our homes. What shifted our perception of cats to make them a popular pet?

We know that domesticated cats are related to wild cats, but theories about when cats first began to live as human companions continue to evolve as new research emerges. Domestic cats are members of the Felidae family, which comprises all the cats—big and small—found on the earth. Pumas, cheetahs, bobcats, lions, tigers, and a few dozen other species are all part of the Felidae family as well. These carnivorous mammals are all descended from the same ancestor—the African wildcat, which still roams parts of Africa and Asia today.

Cats of the Felidae family vary wildly in size, coloring, and shape, but they do have a few things in common. All cats have whiskers, claws (most species have the ability to retract the claws to keep them sharp), and solid, athletic builds. All felid species also have five digits on their front paws and four on their rear paws. These similarities have made it difficult for anthropologists to pinpoint the exact time in history when cats were domesticated, as the fossils of different cat species sometimes look very similar. Theories about the history of the house cat have evolved over the years, but, bit by bit, scientists have put together pieces of the puzzle to form a clear picture.

For a long time, we thought that the ancient Egyptians were the first to embrace cats as pets. The early civilization's dedication to cats was well documented. Cats were often depicted in paintings, sculptures, jewelry, and other art. Historians believe that the ancient

Egyptians perceived cats as magical beings that brought protection and good luck. They believed their deities wanted to embody the traits they associated with cats, such as fertility, guardianship, and ferocity, so some gods chose to inhabit the bodies of cats. Cats were held in such high regard that killing one was a crime punishable by death. It was not unheard of for people to dote on their cats, going as far as adorning them with beautiful gemstones and gold jewelry. Cats that had died were often mummified, and part of the mourning ritual for those who lived in the household involved shaving the eyebrows as a sign of bereavement.

In 1983, archaeologists on the Mediterranean island of Cyprus made an exciting discovery that challenged our understanding of when cats were first domesticated. They unearthed a cat's jawbone that they determined to be eight thousand years old. This dated the fossil back to long before the ancient Egyptians. The archaeologists knew that cats weren't native to Cyprus, so they concluded that cats must have been brought there by boat. This new piece of information put us on a path to a better understanding of the origins of the domestic cat.

In 2004, scientists were again surveying sites in Cyprus. They discovered a burial site in which a human and a cat had been entombed together, along with assorted stones, shells, and tools. The items and placement of the bodies indicated that there was a link between the human and cat, possibly spiritual or indicating companionship. They were able to determine this new discovery was about fifteen hundred years older than the feline jawbone discovered years earlier.

More recent discoveries have uncovered evidence that cats began to live among humans around twelve thousand years ago, in an area of the Middle East where agricultural societies were popping up. The area was named the Fertile Crescent for its especially fertile soil, in which crops grew readily. Humans began to grow more food than they could eat, which sounds like a good problem to have, except that their grain stores were being plundered by rodents. They developed ways to store the surplus food but found the easiest and most effective way to deter the pests was to keep cats around. The cats benefited too, as it provided them with an abundance of prey to hunt. Over time, the cats got used to being around people, and people started to see a more submissive and lovable side to the cats.

When the first European colonists came to the New World, they brought cats with them on their ships. Nicknamed "ship cats," they served a similar purpose—they kept the food safe from rodents. These boat trips across the Atlantic took six to eight weeks, or even longer if the weather wasn't cooperating. It was essential that the food on board—the only food they would have until they reached their destination—did not become contaminated. Cats, once again, did a great job of keeping rats and mice away from the stored provisions.

Once on land, the colonists continued to utilize the cats as rodent control. And, by the late eighteenth century, humans started to appreciate cats for more than just their utility. Cats had proved themselves to be intelligent and loyal, each with its own distinct personality. They began to be more accepted as pets, and by the mid-nineteenth century, they were a well-established presence in many homes. They were so dear to their owners that it was not uncommon for a wealthy cat owner to commission a portrait showing them with their beloved pet!

Since those early days of cat-human camaraderie, humans have come to appreciate cats for more than just their ability to be fluffy, wonderful companions. They are utilized in myriad ways to do a variety of jobs. Many cat careers make use of a cat's rodent-killing skills. In New York City, the bodega cat is ubiquitous; it's very common for a deli to have a resident furball. In exchange for keeping the rats and mice away, the bodega kitty gets shelter, food, and a slew of human neighborhood friends. Similarly, barn cats do the job of keeping a farm vermin-free. For their hard work, they are given carte blanche to roam the fields and outbuildings, living a carefree cat existence.

Cats' contributions, however, have not been limited to rodent control. Over the years, humans have depended on cats to complete a surprising variety of tasks. In the late 1800s, the Belgian Society for Elevation of the Domestic Cat launched a program to teach cats to carry the mail. They sent thirty-seven cats out into the countryside with waterproof bags around their necks to hold messages. The cats all found their way back home within twenty-four hours, giving the program the potential to use cats to increase communication between towns. Unfortunately, the program was short-lived. Although it was possible to teach the cats to deliver the mail, it turned out to be inefficient.

In the 1960s, the CIA experimented with employing cats to spy on the Soviets. They spent $20 million developing the project, which they called Acoustic Kitty. The plan was to outfit a cat with an antenna, radio transmitter, and microphone and train it to follow instructions on where to sit to pick up conversations nearby. However, the first mission failed before they could even test it out. Instead of heading to its target, which was two men conversing in a park, the cat ran into the street. It got hit by a car and that was the end of the Acoustic Kitty program. Cat spies were an interesting idea in theory, but too challenging to properly execute.

It took thousands of years for cats to become domesticated, and in that time many cultures have enjoyed the company of cats. Although the relationship between cats and humans tends to be mutually beneficial, many would agree that the food and shelter we provide are a small price to pay for a cat's companionship and affection. For cat lovers, their kitties are more akin to family members than merely pets.

Aerodynamic Body

Exceptional Hearing

Sharp Vision

Strong Sense
of Smell

Flexible Spine

30 Teeth

Spiky and
Rough Tongue

Sensitive
Whiskers, Noses,
and Paw Pads

Strong Back Legs

Highly Specialized
Paws

THE FELINE FORM

Cats possess an ability to perform Cirque du Soleil–style acrobatics seemingly without effort. Jumping high, balancing on narrow ledges, and sprinting fast are just a few of the feats that we've come to expect from our furry friends. Their stealth moves are the result of specialized physical characteristics, some of which also aid in self-defense, grooming, and eating. Although cats certainly share many of the same bodily systems as other mammals, such as the circulatory, digestive, and respiratory systems, there are also many physical traits that are specific to cats.

Have you ever wondered how cats are able to contort into weird positions, twisting and turning like they're made of rubber? They are extra flexible due to the muscles that hold their spinal columns together. Unlike humans, whose spinal columns are held together with ligaments, cats can lengthen and swivel their vertebrae, giving them a wide range of motion.

Their clavicles and shoulder blades are not attached to other bones; their muscles hold these structures in place. This unique anatomy also allows cats to have a greater freedom of movement, aiding with flexibility and allowing them to fold into tight spaces. Between a cat's vertebrae are discs that cushion impact, allowing them to jump from great heights without injuring their spines. And their spinal vertebrae extend to form their tails, which also play a role in their agility by providing a counterbalance during abrupt movements and when walking on narrow surfaces.

A cat's paws are also highly specialized. They have five digits on their front paws and four on their rear paws; however, an inherited abnormality called poly-dactyly causes some cats to have extra toes. (Polydactyl cats usually have an extra toe on their front paws that makes it look like they are wearing mittens!) The paw pads (or toe beans, as they are affectionately nick-named) provide traction and cushioning, and help reg-ulate temperature. Cats' paws also feature claws that retract. If you've ever had the misfortune of receiving a scratch, you know how sharp a cat's nails can be. Their nails serve a variety of purposes, most importantly to catch prey and to defend themselves from predators. But even indoor cats that don't need to concern themselves with procuring food or fighting off an enemy need their claws to help with balance, climbing, and stretching. The custom of declawing cats has fallen out of favor as we've come to understand the damage it can cause. In many cases, declawing results in pain that persists long after the cat is healed. The best way to manage a cat's nails is to provide them with scratching posts so they can file down their nails as they would in the wild. Trimming nails also prevents them from getting too long or sharp.

If you have ever seen a cat get the zoomies, you know they can run *fast*. With a top speed of about thirty miles per hour, a domestic cat can outrun a tiger! The ability to run superfast is due to a few factors. The fastest cats have an aerodynamic body shape, moving through the air without resistance that would slow them down. They have strong back legs that push them forward with great force. Their flexible spines also help by acting almost like a spring, compressing and then expanding quickly. Although domestic cats are expert sprinters, they're not built for distance running.

In the wild, a cat's main source of food is rodents and other small animals. Adult cats are outfitted with thirty teeth that are specialized to assist with their carnivorous diet. Their front teeth allow them to grasp and tear meat, while their back teeth grind food into small-enough pieces to be swallowed. Their tongues are spiky, covered in tiny barbs that help them get the last remaining bits of meat off bones. They also use their rough tongues to groom and clean their fur.

Cats have the same five senses that we do, each essential to their survival. Sharp vision in low light allows them to see much better than humans in the dark, which comes in handy when these nocturnal animals are out hunting. They also have a wider range of vision than humans, with excellent peripheral sight. Exceptional hearing allows cats to detect frequencies that other animals can't hear at all. Paired with their remarkable ability to accuraely judge speed and distance well, they are uniquely equipped to successfully hunt prey and keep safe from predators. Their senses of taste and smell work together to provide essential information. Although they don't have many taste receptors in their tongues, their strong sense of smell makes up for it. If you've ever seen a cat open its mouth while smelling something, that's because it is using the vomeronasal organ, which sits on the roof of the mouth behind the top teeth and helps the cat smell much more intensely. Since cats use their sense of smell to navigate the world, this is a very useful tool. Lastly, cats have sensitive whiskers, noses, and paw pads that allow them to experience the sense of touch. Whiskers are a type of long, thick hair that grows from a cat's face and legs. They help with sensing nearby objects and gauging whether the cat can fit through a space.

Of all the physical traits fundamental to felines, their fur might be the one humans appreciate most. Petting a cat's plush coat, after all, is one of the major benefits of having a cat. Cats' fur also serves a number of practical purposes. It protects a cat's skin, acting as a shield from the sun (cats can get skin cancer, so it's best to keep them out of the sun to avoid getting sunburns). It serves as a shield to the skin, making injuries less likely. Fur also protects a cat from cold weather, acting like a warm blanket to keep from freezing outside in the winter. (Hairless cats don't benefit from the same protections as furred felines, so they do require special care. They are, however, uniquely velvety and fun to pet!)

Whether living out in the wild or safely inside a home, cats have exceptional features that allow them to thrive.

HOW TO TALK CAT

Cats communicate with each other, and with us, in many ways. They use sounds, movements, and behaviors to get their point across, although we don't always know how to interpret their cues. Sometimes it's quite obvious how a cat is feeling; when your fuzzy friend jumps in your lap to make biscuits while purring, you can be sure your cat is feeling content. But what does it mean when a cat's tail is twitching? Or when a cat slowly bats at an item on a table until it falls off—why do they do that? Why do they do *any* of the odd things they do?

Possibly the most effective tool a cat can use to communicate with other cats is its scent glands. Cats have a number of powerful scent glands on different parts of their bodies. When a cat rubs its mouth, chin, head, butt, or tail on you, it's leaving behind a scent, the purpose of which is twofold. One, leaving its scent, or "marking," is a way to claim its territory. It sends a message to other cats that says, "I was here" or "This is mine." The other purpose of the marking is to create a comfortable, familiar scent in the environment that is calming to the cat. When a cat recognizes the scents in its surroundings, it feels safe. If a new, unfamiliar animal scent is introduced to a cat's household, a cat may feel threatened, which can cause it to spray. Spraying is the release of a heavily scented urine onto whatever items a cat wants to claim. The cat is letting an interloper know it has encroached on their territory.

Cats use their voices to talk to each other and to us. They use a number of sounds to convey different messages. The sound we most associate with cats is the *meow*. Usually, it is the sound that cats make most often, because their *meow* is a general vocalization; it can mean a number of things, such as "Hello" or "I don't like that!" A bossy cat might be telling you to do something. Or it may just be making its presence known. The *hiss* is a much clearer message—it conveys anger, fear, or aggression. Growling and spitting, too, are clear signs that a cat is steaming mad. (You should leave this cat alone!) Purring is a

sign that is somewhat misunderstood. Although it usually means a cat is feeling content, it can also signal that a cat is in pain or feeling stressed and using its *purr* as a self-soothing technique. Not all cats use chirps and trills, but they are most often associated with a mama cat who wants her kittens to follow her. A chirp sounds like a short *peep*, reminiscent of a bird. A trill is a vocalization that a cat doesn't even need to open its mouth to use—it sounds like a *rrrrr* coming from the throat. Chattering is the excited sound a cat sometimes makes when looking at another animal outside a window. Its *ch-ch-ch* is a happy expression that almost sounds like the chattering of teeth. Cats use a howl or yowl to express discomfort or displeasure. Like a prolonged *meow*, it's a sign that a cat is unhappy and is seeking help. Excessive meowing, yowling, and howling call for a trip to the vet to make sure there is no sickness or injury that could be causing pain or discomfort.

You can expect a cat to give you clear physical cues. Its body language will tell you a lot about how it's feeling. A relaxed cat might sit or lie on its back with eyes half-closed and its tail motionless. A scared cat will flatten its ears, sometimes holding its tail between its legs and slinking close to the walls, looking for a place to hide. A playful cat holds its tail up and its ears forward, at times going through the motions of excitedly pouncing and attacking imaginary prey. A twitching tail is a sure sign that a cat is feeling annoyed or aggravated. It's a gentle way of saying "knock it off." A puffed-up tail is a sign that your cat is feeling threatened, so it's trying to make itself look intimidating. An arched back with fur standing up is a clear warning that a cat is feeling angry and may be aggressive. Learning to interpret a cat's body language is a key part of connecting and interacting in a positive way.

Cats have several ways of communicating their love. They may groom the object of their affection, using their tongue to provide a thorough cleaning of the head or ears. (They don't just do this to other cats; beloved human friends are sometimes subject to the tongue bath as well!) Marking is another sign of affection. Those head butts and face rubs leave behind a scent that lets other cats know that a person or object belongs to them. Kneading is a behavior left over from kittenhood, when a cat used its paws to release some of its mother's milk. A kneading cat feels content and happy and wants to express its love. Likewise, a cat on its back with an exposed belly is expressing trust and a feeling of safety. If you're the lucky recipient of any of these behaviors, you can be sure your cat adores you. There are a few things humans can do to communicate their affection toward their cat in a way the cat can understand. The next time you make prolonged eye contact with your kitty, try blinking slowly. Cats themselves use the slow blink when they're relaxed and feeling fondness, so they should understand when you reciprocate. Engaging in active play and providing interactive toys improves a cat's quality of life and lets it know you care. Lastly, give your cat lots of comfortable spots around the house to perch and recline. They will appreciate these signs of respect and devotion.

When cats misbehave (or act in a way that we interpret negatively), they are also conveying information.

Scratching furniture is not a specific attempt at defacing your property; it's their way of filing their nails, as they would do to a tree in the wild. Providing a scratching post can help direct a cat to the proper place for nail maintenance. (A cat that enjoys catnip might be more inclined to use their scratching post if it has been rubbed with the enchanting plant.) Chewing inappropriate objects is usually the result of boredom, and should be curbed before accidental ingestion, which can cause blockages in the intestines. Cats that poop outside the litter box are expressing their displeasure about something. Barring illness or old age, it could be that the litter box is not as clean as the cat would prefer. Or perhaps something has changed at home, like a new pet or even new furniture. Cats are not usually big fans of change, so even a minor shift can cause annoyance. If your cat brings you a surprise in the form of a dead bird or rodent, in its mind it is giving you a precious gift! Though it may be disgusting to the human recipient, it is a meaningful declaration of a cat's affection. Aw!

Cat behavior is sometimes confounding to even the most knowledgeable cat owners. Have you ever had a cat make eye contact while slowly batting an object off a surface and onto the floor? It feels like utter lunacy, but it's most likely just a bid for your attention. What about when you find your cat squeezed into a spot that is almost too small for it when it has endless comfortable spots around the house? This is a cat's instinct to hide in an enclosed space to keep safe from predators, as it would do in the wild. And why do cats get the middle-of-the-night zoomies when you're trying to get some rest? Cats are nocturnal, so that is the time they would naturally hunt for food. It might feel like a personal affront, but it's just the cat's instincts taking over, as is so often the case when a cat does something you don't understand. The next time you're faced with unfavorable behavior from your cat, ask yourself what purpose it might have served in the wild. It just might improve the way you relate to and communicate with your cat.

FAMOUS FELINES

Countless cats throughout history have made a lasting impact; their stories sometimes resonate and stick with us throughout our lifetimes. Whether remembered for their good looks, funny personality, or memorable misdeeds, some cats just have a way of working their way into our hearts. Some of these cats are characters from TV shows and movies. Others we discovered on social media or in a classic book from childhood. Who would you add to this list?

🐾 🐾 🐾 GARFIELD 🐾 🐾 🐾

You may know Garfield as the lasagna-loving, Monday-hating, dry-humored orange cat from the long-running *Garfield* comic strip. Creator Jim Davis felt that cats were underrepresented in the Sunday funnies and based his main character on all the cats he had known throughout his childhood. Known for his cynicism and laziness, this chubby tabby first appeared in newspapers in 1978 to mixed reactions. After only months of running it, the *Chicago Sun-Times* dropped the comic from its pages. In response, fans sent more than a thousand angry letters to the paper, causing them to reconsider their decision. *Garfield* fandom continued to grow and reach new audiences with countless television specials, movies, books, and merchandise. In the 1980s, demand was high for Garfield products. In addition to the usual T-shirts, mugs, and character goods, iconic Garfield phone and car-window plushes were everywhere. In 2015, the *Guinness Book of World Records* named *Garfield* the most widely syndicated comic strip in the world. Today, it runs in over twenty-four hundred newspapers worldwide!

🐾 🐾 🐾 FELIX THE CAT 🐾 🐾 🐾

In the early 1920s, a black-and-white cartoon cat gave silent film star Charlie Chaplin a run for his money. Over a hundred short films starring the delightfully mischievous Felix were shown in movie theaters all over the world. Audiences fell in love with Felix, who became the very first animated film star. His popularity continued when, in 1923, *Felix the Cat* was adapted into a weekly comic strip that was published in over 250 newspapers throughout the world. By 1927, Felix was a household name. He has the distinction of being the first cartoon character to be made into a balloon in the Macy's Thanksgiving Day Parade. He was also the very first image to be transmitted in a television broadcast! In 1928, a rotating statue of Felix was used as a test in NBC's first broadcast. But that was just the beginning of Felix's TV career; at the end of the 1950s, Paramount created the *Felix the Cat* TV show that played in reruns for decades, bringing the joy of Felix to a whole new generation.

🐾 🐾 🐾 CHESHIRE CAT 🐾 🐾 🐾

The well-known children's book *Alice's Adventures in Wonderland* by Lewis Carroll features many unusual and intriguing characters, including a murderous Queen, the always-in-a-rush White Rabbit, and a melancholy Mock Turtle. But perhaps the most enduring character after Alice herself is the mysterious Cheshire Cat, who appears and disappears in an unpredictable fashion throughout the book. In the 1951 Disney film *Alice in Wonderland*, which was based on the book, the

Cheshire Cat is shown as a perpetually grinning, pink-and-purple-striped trickster. Quick to offer help, then confuse Alice with his clever wordplay, he is probably best remembered for his perpetual grin, which sometimes lingered long after the rest of him had disappeared. Rumor has it that the Disney version of the Cheshire Cat was a British Shorthair, though of course the animators took some liberties with its coloring.

🐾 🐾 🐾 SALEM SABERHAGEN 🐾 🐾 🐾

You might know Salem Saberhagen as the chatty black cat from the 1990s sitcom *Sabrina the Teenage Witch*. He was, of course, not your average cat. In fact, he wasn't even a cat, but a five-hundred-year-old warlock whose punishment for trying to take over the world was to reside in the body of a cat for one hundred years. Sent to live with the wacky Hilda Spellman in the mortal realm, Salem also shares a house with Zelda, Hilda's sister, and their niece Sabrina. Throughout the seven seasons of the series, he gets himself into a bunch of trouble, but also offers Sabrina endless guidance and loyalty.

The character of Salem Saberhagen first appeared in Archie Comics in the early 1960s. He was depicted as an orange cat who didn't talk. After his reimagining for *Sabrina the Teenage Witch*, his strong personality and sense of humor became the cornerstone of the character in the many future spin-off shows and comics.

🐾 🐾 🐾 GRUMPY CAT 🐾 🐾 🐾

In 2012, a photo of a cat with a cranky expression was posted to a Reddit group and the world was never the same. Originally met with cynicism and disbelief that the image was not Photoshopped, the owner proved the cat's authenticity by posting a ten-second video to YouTube. Within days, Grumpy Cat, as she became known, was a worldwide sensation. People couldn't get enough of her adorably sour face, which was caused by an underbite and feline dwarfism. She inspired countless memes and collected millions of likes and follows online. Although she was actually named Tardar Sauce, her owners leaned into the public's fascination with her perpetually angry face. Before long, you could buy books, calendars, home goods, shirts, figurines, and a slew of other Grumpy Cat merchandise. She even had a fragrance called Kitten Fur! Unfortunately, Tardar Sauce passed away at only seven years old from complications of a urinary tract infection. Her legacy, however, lives on, and she is still inspiring memes and gaining new fans to this day.

🐾 🐾 🐾 LIL BUB 🐾 🐾 🐾

Lil BUB was a small cat with a huge impact. Born in a shed in rural Indiana, she was the smallest of her litter and would not have survived without human intervention. She was born with a condition that caused a number of physical irregularities, many of which contributed to her especially cute appearance. She did not have teeth and her jaw was undersized, making her tongue stick out permanently (and adorably). She was also very small, only around four pounds, and she had an extra toe on each paw. Lil BUB's owner started a Tumblr in 2011 to share her with the world, but it wasn't until a photo of her made it to Reddit in 2012 that she became an Internet sensation. Lil BUB got busy with appearances and projects, spreading her message of accepting people's differences and helping others. Among her many remarkable endeavors, she starred in a documentary called *Lil BUB and Friendz* in 2013. That same year she also published a book, called *Lil BUB's Lil Book*, filled with pictures chronicling her extraordinary life. But Lil BUB's most impressive work was her mission to spread information about special-needs animals and raise money for their care. Overall, she raised about $1 million, roughly half of which was for Lil BUB's BIG Fund for the ASPCA. Sadly, she passed away on December 1, 2019, leaving a legacy of animal welfare and compassion for others.

🐾 🐾 🐾 NALA CAT 🐾 🐾 🐾

With 4.4 million followers and counting, Nala Cat is the most famous cat on Instagram. Fans are drawn to her sweet blue eyes and affable nature, as depicted in photos of her everyday life posted online. Started as a way for her owner to share images of her precious cat with family in Thailand, Nala's page didn't get much attention at first. That is until she was featured on Instagram's "popular" page. Rabid fans clamored for merchandise, and brands approached the cat with sponsorship opportunities. Nala became the first feline influencer! She even launched her own brand of cat food, called Love, Nala. Wanting to use her newfound fame for good, Nala's owners began promoting causes that were near and dear to them. Nala had been adopted at about five months old from a high-kill shelter in Los Angeles, so they worked to spread awareness about animal adoption. They also promoted the importance of spaying and neutering pets to avoid overpopulation.

These days, Nala has a pack of furry friends—adopted siblings Stella, Steve, Apollo, Coffee, Luna, and Spencer (the only dog!) each have their own Internet presence. Together, they support the Paw Project, a nonprofit that aims to educate pet owners about the cruelty of declawing.

🐾 🐾 🐾 MR. BIGGLESWORTH 🐾 🐾 🐾

Have you ever seen the popular meme of a hairless cat who appears to be frozen with its mouth open and a caption that reads "It's frickin' cold in here!"? That's Mr. Bigglesworth, from the Austin Powers movie franchise!

In the three movies, Mr. Bigglesworth is the trusted companion of the villainous Dr. Evil. He was born a fluffy white cat, but lost all his fur after being cryogenically frozen for thirty years. (The character is a spoof of the white Persian cat owned by the villain Blofeld from the James Bond series.) The role of Mr. Bigglesworth was played by a purebred Sphynx named Ted Nudegent. The cat actor received special training to be able to play the part—he had to be taught to remain calm during scenes where other characters are yelling and gesticulating, which is not an easy feat for a cat! It helped that Ted Nudegent was so fond of Mike Myers (the actor who portrayed Dr. Evil) that the cat would fall asleep in his lap. Quite adorable, but probably not fun for the crew, as it caused filming delays.

Mr. Bigglesworth fans are still hoping for a fourth Austin Powers movie one day. In the meantime, anyone jonesing for more Mr. Bigglesworth in their life will have to settle for a hat, T-shirt, stuffed animal, or a repeat viewing of one of the Austin Powers movies. And if that doesn't suffice, one can always find a vintage Mr. Bigglesworth talking doll on eBay!

🐾 🐾 🐾 SHOW CATS 🐾 🐾 🐾

There are plenty more cats of note beyond the delightful pop culture icons above. Since the late nineteenth century, cat shows have given breeders and cat owners the opportunity to participate in competitions that award titles to cats that closely exhibit their breed's standards. The very first cat show took place in 1871 at the Crystal Palace in London. Cats were not popular pets at the time, but the organizers managed to round up enough pedigreed and common cats to put on a show. The cats were separated by breed and size and judged on a set of standards. The show was a surprise success, bringing in crowds and generating interest in an animal that many thought of as a mere rodent-control measure. Enthusiasm and affection for cats grew and breeding programs were developed. This led to an increase in demand for more cat shows.

A few years after the first cat show in London, interest in cats spread to the United States. In 1899, the Chicago Cat Club was formed, ushering in the practice of registering domestic cats and tracking the lineage of various breeds. In 1906, the main cat registry of the time, the American Cat Association, splintered and produced the Cat Fanciers' Association (CFA), which became the largest and best-known registering association. Today, the CFA hosts cat shows, creates breed standards, trains show judges, and offers guidelines to breeders. The CFA also offers certified pedigree lists, tracing a registered cat's lineage back three to six generations.

A BREED APART

Over forty-five breeds of domestic cat are recognized by the major cat registries. Each breed has its own set of physical traits and personality quirks. The most common type of cat, however, is not a recognized breed at all. It is the domestic shorthair, also known as the common cat. A mix of breeds, the domestic shorthair is not bred to a set of standards, as other recognized breeds are. They are, in fact, not bred at all; they're a result of natural reproduction between two other domestic shorthairs. The only physical trait they all have in common is their short hair. (The domestic longhair, similarly, is a common cat that has long hair. They are far less common than the domestic shorthair.) The rest of the domestic shorthair's characteristics are the result of a random and broad lineage that mixes many different breeds.

You will have no problem finding an exceptional kitty at your local shelter. You may be familiar with the "Adopt, Don't Shop" campaign, which raises awareness about the hundreds of thousands of shelter animals that are euthanized each year and the problems with purchasing animals created in inhumane puppy and kitten mills. At any given time, there are thousands of adorable, healthy cats waiting for their forever homes. Cats of all ages (including kittens!), colors, and temperaments are always available if you're looking to grow your family. Giving a shelter cat a home is a worthwhile commitment. You'll be giving a cat a chance at having a good life that it might not have otherwise. And knowing that you made a difference in an animal's life is an invaluable gift, both to yourself and the lucky kitty.

If you're looking for a particular breed, you may need to go to a breeder. There are many reasons a person might seek out a unique breed. When you purchase a cat from a breeder, you're getting a pet that is likely to have certain desired traits and a predictable appearance. But there are also drawbacks to getting a cat through a breeder. For one, there's the cost. A bred cat can cost thousands of dollars—more for rare breeds or ones from distinguished bloodlines. They can also have health challenges or even shorter life spans as result of in-breeding. It's crucial to research a breeder before working with them. A legitimate breeder will be registered with a well-known cat breed registry. The cattery should also be able to provide, as part of the cost, a pedigree with the genealogy of the purchased kitten. Be diligent to avoid supporting a backyard breeder and potentially getting a cat that will have health problems down the road.

On the following pages, learn about some of the most common cat breeds, including details about what they look like, where they came from, and their typical behaviors.

ABYSSINIAN

SIZE: medium	COAT: medium length, silky

COLOR: ruddy, cinnamon, blue, fawn

TEMPERAMENT: active, curious

If you're looking for a cat with a quiet temperament and a regal disposition, an Abyssinian might be right for you. Slender and agile, these long-legged felines are known to be intelligent, curious, and playful. Bursting with energy, they enjoy climbing, jumping, and investigating. Although they tend to be independent, they do enjoy having a cat companion to help them keep busy. They can be shy with strangers, but they don't hesitate to cuddle up with a familiar person.

Abys, as they are often called, have medium-length coats. They are usually a reddish-brown color, though they sometimes come in shades of red, blue, or fawn. Their coats are "ticked," meaning some of their individual strands of hair have bands of black or brown. Their striking, almond-shaped eyes are gold or green.

Abyssinians resemble the cats of ancient Egypt, as depicted in statues and art from that time. Cats were held in high regard, and many of their deities were sculpted and painted with cat heads. Despite the resemblance, there is growing evidence that Abyssinians did not originate in Egypt. Genetic testing has revealed that the breed can be traced back to Southeast Asia and was likely brought to Europe by British and Dutch traders. The first of the breed was imported to the United States in 1900, and by the 1930s they were being brought from Britain to be bred. Today, they are one of the world's most popular cat breeds and a popular contestant in cat shows.

BALINESE

SIZE: medium	COAT: medium length, silky
COLOR: seal point, chocolate point, blue point, lilac point	
TEMPERAMENT: loyal, outgoing	

The perfect cat for a person of refined taste, the Balinese is known for its beauty, outgoing personality, intelligence, and curiosity. Not recognized as a breed until 1979, its exact history is unknown. We do know that it happens to share the same traits as the Siamese with one exception: the length of its coat. Given the striking similarities, it is likely that the Balinese is simply a Siamese with a longer, lush coat!

The Balinese gets its name from the grace and elegance of the dancers on the Indonesian island of Bali. Indeed, the cats are agile and dignified, with long back legs that make them great jumpers. They are medium in size, with a wedge-shaped head, large triangular ears, and sapphire-blue eyes. In addition to their luxurious fur, they have fanciful floofy tails. They come in a range of colors (the same colors as the Siamese!).

This is the perfect breed for someone looking for a companion. Balinese love their owners dearly and are very devoted pets. They want to be with their humans as much as possible and will follow them around the house. These goofballs are very chatty, making them a nice breed for someone who enjoys carrying on long, animated conversations with their cat. They get along nicely with people, other cats, and dogs. And they can be trained to do tricks!

Requiring quite a bit of attention, this breed is not the best for someone who isn't home a lot or prefers an easygoing cat. One thing to keep in mind is that Balinese love to climb. Don't be surprised if you find them scaling your furniture to the highest points in your home. Although they are not the easiest cats to care for, if you're willing to put in the work, you will be rewarded with a devoted companion and a fun-loving friend.

BENGAL

SIZE: medium to large	COAT: short, soft

COLOR: a wide variety of patterns, including brown tabby, blue tabby, seal lynx point, seal sepia tabby, blue lynx point, blue mink tabby, seal silver lynx point, seal silver sepia tabby, blue silver lynx point, and blue silver mink tabby

TEMPERAMENT: affectionate, intelligent

The Bengal, with its large frame and spotted or marbled coat, is the result of breeding a domestic cat with a small Asian leopard cat. It was developed in 1963 to meet the demand for wild cats to be kept as pets—an idea that might seem fun, but isn't safe for the average household!

Although Bengals have a look more wild than some other breeds, their personalities are pure joy. They have energy to spare and are highly curious and intelligent. They love attention and are happy to climb and play all day. Many Bengals love water and will happily splash in a faucet stream or the water left after a shower. Not likely to spend much time in its owner's lap, a Bengal would rather be outside chasing birds (or watching them from a window) and climbing as high as it can.

Bengals come in a wide variety of colors and patterns. Some appear to sparkle in the sun! This is the result of a gene that gives the coat a glittery, iridescent sheen in certain light. The short, soft coat of a Bengal is easy to care for—weekly brushing is enough to keep the dust bunnies at bay.

This breed is best in a household where there is someone home much of the time. Without interaction,

Bengals can get bored and look for ways to entertain themselves. They may become destructive or show anxious behaviors, like overgrooming or repeatedly licking themselves in one spot. Properly cared for, however, Bengals are delightfully playful and interactive. They tend to respond well to training and enjoy the challenge of learning new tricks.

BOMBAY

SIZE: medium	COAT: medium length
COLOR: black	
TEMPERAMENT: active, curious	

The closest you will get to having a pet panther, the Bombay is the result of crossing a Burmese with a black American Shorthair. These medium-sized cats are solidly built, with a muscular frame and soft black coat with a sheen that looks like patent leather. Their gold, almond-shaped eyes are quite striking next to their jet-black fur.

Bombays are known for being friendly, social, and easygoing. They get along well with other pets and new people, although they will insist on being the cat-in-charge in a home with other felines. Happy to curl up in your lap for a snooze, they also love playing active games like fetch and can be trained to walk on a leash. They also love being the center of attention and will want to be involved in whatever you're doing. It's not uncommon for a Bombay to insert itself into its owner's activities, which could mean you have a cat sprawled out on your laptop while you're trying to work or slinking around your feet during your morning yoga routine. These highly intelligent cats need stimulation to keep from getting bored. Puzzles, toys, and interactive play will help keep a Bombay entertained and happy.

BRITISH SHORTHAIR

SIZE: medium to large	**COAT:** short, dense

COLOR: white, black, blue, cream, various tabby patterns, tortoiseshell, calico, and bicolor

TEMPERAMENT: affectionate, loyal

Believed to be the oldest cat breed in England, the British Shorthair has a lineage that goes way back to the cats of ancient Rome. When the Romans invaded the British, they brought cats with them to help protect their food stores. Those cats lived on the streets until the breeding of cats became a common practice in Victorian England.

With its large, stocky body, dense fur, and round head, the British Shorthair is like a teddy bear come to life. The breed is medium to large in size, with a short, thick tail and squat legs. You can find these cats in a wide variety of colors and patterns, but blue is the most common color, and the one generally associated with the breed. No matter the color, their fur is plush and extra-soft. There is a longhair version of the British Shorthair called the British Longhair. Their only distinction is the length of their coats.

Nowadays, the British Shorthair is the most common cat in the United Kingdom. They are sought out for their relaxed, affable demeanor and their affinity for humans. They are known for being adaptable and able to live with people of all ages and pets of other species as well. These are not the most athletic cats and may even seem clumsy at times, but what they lack in agility, they make up for by being top-notch lap cats. British Shorthairs love their human companions and give affection freely.

BURMESE

SIZE: medium	COAT: short, silky
COLOR: sable, champagne, blue, and platinum	
TEMPERAMENT: friendly, affectionate	

Burmese are first and foremost people-cats, meaning they love their people deeply and wish to spend as much time as possible alongside their human companions. A Burmese will follow you from room to room, taking every opportunity to jump into your lap, rub up against your legs, or cuddle with you under the covers. They have big, joyous personalities and love playtime. You'll never have a dull moment with a Burmese. You'll also never have a quiet moment—these chatty kitties are very vocal, with deep raspy voices.

Burmese have silky, glossy coats and wide, saucer-like eyes set far apart on rounded heads. They are surprisingly heavy for their size, which is the result of their athletic, muscular bodies on small frames.

Burmese do best in a home where they are not left alone a lot. They crave company, attention, and interaction. Doing puzzles and learning tricks are surefire ways to keep a Burmese occupied.

All Burmese cats are descended from the same cat—a brown kitty from Burma named Wong Mau. Brought to the United States in 1930, she was bred with Siamese cats. Some of her kittens looked just like her, and others looked just like their Siamese fathers. A third group of kittens had blended features, and these would become the standard for what we now know as the Burmese.

CALICO

SIZE: varies	COAT: varies
COLOR: white with patches of two other colors	
TEMPERAMENT: varies	

You won't find an entry for the calico in a list of official cat breeds. "Calico" does not refer to a specific breed; rather it describes a type of coloring. Calicos have tri-color fur—they are usually mostly white, with patches of two more colors, often orange and black. They are frequently mistaken for tortoiseshell cats, but "torties" have very little, if any, white fur, and are predominantly brown with different-color streaks.

Calicos do not have a standard size, coat length, or temperament. These details will be determined by the cat's breed. Many breeds exhibit the calico color-ing, including the Persian, Japanese Bobtail, American Shorthair, and Maine Coon, to name just a few.

Most calicos are female. This is because the X chro-mosome carries a gene for fur color. For a cat to have orange and black fur, it would need to have two X chro-mosomes (one for each color), which only female mam-mals have. White fur is actually an absence of color and a result of a gene mutation. This phenomenon is called piebalding, and it occurs in several animal species.

In 2001, the state of Maryland picked the calico as their official state cat. They chose it because it matched the colors of Maryland's state bird, the Baltimore oriole, which also has colors of white, orange, and black. (The state's official insect is the Baltimore checkerspot butterfly. Can you guess its colors?)

CHARTREUX

SIZE: females are medium; males are large

COAT: medium-short with a woolly texture

COLOR: a range of blue-gray colors

TEMPERAMENT: quiet, sweet

Hailing from France, the Chartreux was first introduced to the United States in 1970. It is still a relatively new breed, having only been recognized by the Cat Fanciers' Association (CFA) in 1987. The CFA is one of a few registries of pedigreed cats, and they set the standards for what is expected from each breed. In addition to the physical traits of the Chartreux, they note that the "qualities of strength, intelligence, and amenability… should be evident in all exhibition animals and preserved through careful selection."

Indeed, the Chartreux is known for being smart and for having an agreeable personality. They make friends easily and will bond with other pets and humans in a household. Their favorite activity is lounging in their human's lap, but they are quick to show off athletic prowess when playing or chasing rodents. (They are excellent mousers.) Although generally quiet, they might chirp when they need your attention.

Chartreux have round, stocky bodies that sit atop short legs. Their rounded faces feature a smiling expression that conveys the cat's inherent pleasant nature. The woolly gray fur of a Chartreux needs to be maintained by combing, not brushing. Most of the year, weekly combing is sufficient, but during the few times a year that they blow out their undercoat, daily grooming is best.

DEVON REX

SIZE: medium	**COAT:** short, dense, wavy
COLOR: a wide range of colors and patterns	
TEMPERAMENT: active, intelligent	

The Devon Rex has a look all its own, with wide eyes, high cheekbones, a wavy coat, and supersize low-set ears. The breed originated in Devon, England, in 1960. As the story goes, a woman named Beryl Cox had a female cat who was impregnated by a feral male. The litter contained one brownish-black kitten that had wavy fur like its father. Named Kirlee, Beryl recognized its unique coat, which she thought resembled a Cornish Rex. Although Kirlee did have some characteristics of a Cornish Rex, further testing revealed that its wavy coat was a result of a gene that had not yet been documented. Cats with this gene, called Devon Gene 2, were then bred to secure the future of this new breed. Nowadays, all Devon Rex have a family tree that leads back to Kirlee.

The Devon Rex is a sought-after breed for many reasons. They are known for being excellent family pets, able to get along with children and other animals. Their outgoing nature and acceptance of new people make them a good choice for a therapy cat. They are trainable and thrive when given attention. Many families choose a Devon Rex because they are purported to be hypoallergenic, but this claim has been disputed (the dander that causes allergies is not in the hair itself; rather it is in a cat's skin). Their rippled fur is, however, easy to groom and they don't shed much.

With their highly intelligent and playful nature, the Devon Rex is best suited for people who have the time and resources to provide the stimulation and interaction that they crave. Given the opportunity, a Devon Rex will be your very best friend and an invaluable companion—always at your side, ready to play or cuddle.

EGYPTIAN MAU

SIZE: medium	COAT: medium length, spotted
COLOR: silver, bronze, smoke	
TEMPERAMENT: gentle, athletic	

With its lithe, long body and well-developed muscles, the Egyptian Mau is an athletic wonder. Able to run at speeds of thirty miles per hour, it is the fastest breed of domestic cat. Physical prowess, however, is just one of many of the Egyptian Mau's assets. This breed is known for its exceptional personality; owners say that the cat's loyalty, intelligence, and charming nature are unmatched. The Mau is also an extremely striking animal with almond-shaped green eyes, an elegant gait, and glossy fur with a gorgeous spotted pattern. It is the only breed of domestic cat to have naturally occurring spots.

Shy with strangers, the Egyptian Mau is happiest when spending time with familiar people. Although these cats can be slow to warm up, once they are comfortable, they are quite playful and outgoing, with loads of curiosity. The breed is known for being very interactive and lively. Maus love to climb and will quickly ascend to the highest spot in any room, so perches and cat trees are essential.

The Egyptian Mau is believed to hail from Egypt. Its unique spots and markings match the depiction of cats in ancient Egyptian artwork. Maus weren't bred until the 1950s and were not recognized as a breed by American cat associations until the late 1970s. These days, if you are looking for a Mau kitten, you will likely have to wait for one to become available. Very few end up in shelters, so working with a reputable breeder may be the best option.

EXOTIC SHORTHAIR

SIZE: medium to large	COAT: short, plush
COLOR: a wide range of colors and patterns, including brown, fawn, blue, tortoiseshell, and tabby	
TEMPERAMENT: peaceful, loyal, affectionate	

The perfect cat for someone who wants the look of a Persian without the intense grooming routine, the Exotic Shorthair—or just "Exotic" as it is also known—is one of the most popular cat breeds. In 2021, the Cat Fanciers' Association named it third in a list of the top cat breeds, one spot ahead of its long-haired counterpart.

With its wide eyes, snub nose, round head, and large body, it would be indistinguishable from a Persian if it were not for its short, plush, easier-to-maintain coat. (Needing only weekly grooming, Exotics' coats require far less attention than the daily brushing that keeps the Persian's coat tangle-free.) Exotics are large-boned with a rounded midsection and sizable head. They have sturdy, short legs and a somewhat short tail. Due to their flat faces, these cats sometimes have breathing problems. They also do not do well in hot weather, so care must be taken to make sure that the temperature at home remains comfortable.

Just as the Exotic mirrors the appearance of a Persian, its personality is also similar. Quiet and peaceful, this agreeable cat doesn't need much to be content. They can be playful and will excitedly bat a toy around the house, but they are also happy to relax and cuddle with their person on the couch. Males tend to be more affectionate than females of this breed, but no matter which gender, they are exceptionally sweet and loyal companions.

HIMALAYAN

SIZE: medium to large	COAT: long
COLOR: a variety of colorpoints, including seal, blue, chocolate, and lilac	
TEMPERAMENT: quiet, easygoing	

Much like the Exotic Shorthair, the Himalayan is similar to a Persian but with a different coat pattern. Himalayans, or "Himmys," have lighter-colored bodies with darker colors on the feet, face, ears, and tail. Known as point coloration, this contrast in colors is most often associated with Siamese cats (and in fact the Siamese was used in early breeding programs to perfect the pattern the breeders were seeking). Himmys also come in the same coat colors and with the same bright blue eyes as the Siamese.

Like the Persian, the Himalayan is medium to large in size, with long hair, a snub nose, and big, round eyes. Its coat requires the same maintenance as the Persian, with daily grooming essential to avoiding mats and tangles. The Himalayan also has the Persian's gentle, pleasant demeanor. They are happy to enjoy some quiet cuddling in a lap, but they also enjoy a rousing session with a feather-on-a-string toy or a stuffed mouse.

Whether the Himalayan is a breed of its own or a type of Persian has been hotly debated, with no consensus reached. Either way, it has no bearing on the Himalayan's popularity, which continues to climb.

MAINE COON

SIZE: medium to large	COAT: long, shaggy
COLOR: a wide range of colors and patterns, including black, white, tabby, bicolor, and parti-color	
TEMPERAMENT: friendly, social, vocal	

The Maine Coon is believed to be the oldest cat breed native to the United States. No one knows for sure the origins of the breed, although there have been multiple theories. We know for sure that, despite what you may have heard, the Maine Coon is not the result of a cat-racoon dalliance. It is more likely that the Maine Coon is the result of domestic shorthaired cats that mated with longhaired foreigners brought to New England on ships from overseas. The earliest record we have of the breed is from a cat show in 1861. By 1895, a Maine Coon had won the title of Best Cat at the National Cat Show at Madison Square Garden. With its muscular frame, formidable size, and tough, shaggy mane, this breed was well suited for its original purpose: working on the farm. Even during the harsh Maine winters, the Maine Coon could withstand the cold.

Nowadays, the Maine Coon consistently tops the lists of the most popular cat breeds, and for good reason. These friendly and sociable cats make excellent family pets and wonderful companions. They don't require too much attention or specialized care, making them an easy breed to own. Despite their long hair, their coats are easy to maintain—weekly grooming is sufficient since their fur isn't prone to matting or tangles. And with such stunning, silky long hair, it's easy to imagine how lovely it would be to have a Maine Coon around to cuddle. They are also excellent conversationalists, inclined to trill, chirp, and chatter to express their feelings to their owners.

MANX

SIZE: medium	COAT: long or short

COLOR: a wide range of colors and patterns, including black, blue, red, tabby, calico, and tortoiseshell

TEMPERAMENT: playful, gentle

Hailing from the Isle of Man in the Irish Sea, the Manx is one of the oldest cat breeds. With a sturdy frame and keen intellect, they were utilized on the island as working cats. In 1906, when the Cat Fanciers' Association was started, the Manx was one of the originating breeds.

Best known for something it *doesn't* have, the Manx is tailless. Likely a genetic mutation from inbreeding early in the Manx's history, the degree of taillessness varies. Some have absolutely no tail, just a smooth, rounded rump. Cats with no tails whatsoever are called rumpies. A rumpy riser is a Manx with barely a stub of a tail. Only rumpies and rumpy risers are allowed to compete in the championship classes at certain cat shows. Surprisingly, due to a peculiar genetic quirk, two tailless Manx cats sometimes produce kittens with tails. Even stranger, a single litter can contain Manx kittens with tails of all different lengths!

The Manx is a sturdy cat with an athleticism that allows it to jump high and pivot in a flash. As a pet, the Manx has the ideal mix of qualities: playful, affectionate, smart, and loyal. You will never be bored with a Manx around.

MUNCHKIN

SIZE: small	COAT: long or short
COLOR: a wide variety of colors and patterns	
TEMPERAMENT: outgoing, playful	

It's easy to see how the Munchkin got its name. Due to a genetic abnormality, Munchkins have short legs and go through life a bit lower to the ground than other breeds. (Think of a Corgi or a Dachshund and you'll get the idea.) Despite their shortcomings, the Munchkin is as friendly as they come, playing well with kids, dogs, and other cats. They are supersmart and enjoy interactive play. They may not be able to jump very high, but they make up for it with their sky-high energy and enthusiasm.

The Munchkin is sometimes affectionately given the nickname "magpie," after the curious birds that allegedly enjoy stealing and hoarding shiny trinkets. True to its nickname, the Munchkin has been known to swipe and hide various items. If you have a Munchkin, you will want to keep your valuables tucked away safely.

Given that the Munchkin's genetic irregularity is specific to its limb length, the breed does not have standards by which they are measured. Breeders use a technique called outcrossing, or mating two different breeds, to ensure the offspring's genetic health and avoid the defects that can occur with inbreeding. The result is that the Munchkins produced have all different colors, patterns, coats, and coat lengths.

A relatively new type of cat, the Munchkin wasn't recognized as a breed until 1983. Although some of the well-known cat organizations now acknowledge the Munchkin as a breed, there are many that, to this day, do not. Nevertheless, the Munchkin continues to have an undeniable appeal and scores of steadfast devotees.

NORWEGIAN FOREST CAT

SIZE: large	COAT: thick, long

COLOR: a variety of colors and patterns, including black, red, tortoiseshell, tabby, smoke, and calico

TEMPERAMENT: laid-back, sweet

At first glance, one might confuse a Norwegian Forest cat for a Maine Coon. Indeed, both breeds are large and sturdy, with impressive long hair and fluffy tails. But look closer and you'll see subtle differences. The Norwegian Forest cat, or Wegie, has eyes that are large and almond-shaped, while the Maine Coon's are more rounded and gold or green in color. Norwegian Forest cats also have heads that are more of a triangular shape than the Maine Coon's rectangular-shaped head. Both breeds are built to withstand freezing temperatures. The Wegie is the official cat of Norway, where the winters are long and cold.

As a pet, the Wegie is an easygoing, social cat with moderate activity needs. It gets along with other animals and develops a strong bond with its humans. Although fairly independent, these cats do enjoy quiet moments spent in their loved ones' laps. They also love playtime and will happily take an opportunity to chase and jump. They adore climbing, so a tall cat tree—the higher the better—will keep a Wegie happy. Unlike those of some other longhaired breeds, their luscious coats only require brushing once a week, or twice in the spring when they lose their heavy winter undercoats.

The friendly Norwegian Forest cat is a wonderful companion with a sweet disposition. Take the time to teach your Wegie tricks and you will be rewarded with its attention and affection.

OCICAT

SIZE: medium to large	COAT: short with a spotted pattern
COLOR: a wide variety of colors with distinct, sharply contrasting spots	
TEMPERAMENT: vocal, active, affectionate	

Sturdy and large, with a muscular build, the Ocicat gives off the impression of having great power and strength. Its smooth, shiny coat is short and spotted like a leopard's. It's no wonder cat novices sometimes question whether the Ocicat is domesticated—it looks remarkably like a wild cat! In fact, it was named for its resemblance to the ocelot.

It's no accident that the Ocicat looks the way it does. The breed was conceived by interbreeding the Abyssinian, American Shorthair, and Siamese. The result, after many years of development, is truly remarkable. The Ocicat is the only cat bred to produce a domestic cat with the physical features of a wild one.

Although the Ocicat has the look of an untamed creature, its personality is anything but unruly. Able to befriend people of all ages and pets of various species, the breed thrives as a family pet. It loves its people and lives for their attention and affection. Even strangers are greeted with warmth; it's not unusual for an Ocicat to choose to sit in the lap of a brand-new friend.

An Ocicat does best in an active home; they love the hustle and bustle of a busy household. Spending a lot of time alone is not ideal for this sociable, energetic breed. The best home for an Ocicat is one where it receives a good deal of interaction, love, attention, and opportunities to explore and play.

PERSIAN

SIZE: medium to large	COAT: long and thick

COLOR: a wide variety of colors and patterns, including chocolate, lilac, tabby, calico, tortoiseshell, bicolor, and parti-color

TEMPERAMENT: calm, gentle

Medium to large in size, with a strong, stocky body; long, thick coat; and extravagant, downy tail, the Persian has been a sought-after cat breed for over a century. Prized for its beauty, the breed has a distinctive snub nose, small ears, and round eyes that give it a most adorable expression.

Persians have been a mainstay of cat shows and competitions since 1871, when a Persian was named Best in Show for the first, but certainly not the last, time. When the Cat Fanciers' Association was formed in 1906, the Persian was one of the first registered breeds. More recently, the organization gave the Persian fourth place for top cat breeds of 2021.

The Persian is well suited to an owner who has extra time to properly care for and maintain the cat's long coat. Daily brushing and weekly baths will keep its coat clean and prevent tangles and hairballs. It is also recommended that Persians have their faces washed daily, as their large eyes tend to tear, which can result in staining if not addressed. Some Persians, especially ones with extremely flat faces, may have trouble breathing, which in turn can affect their ability to run, jump, and play.

Although this breed may be high-maintenance in terms of its appearance, the Persian is anything but when it comes to disposition. Persians are easygoing and gentle lap cats with a penchant for cuddling. With their quiet and calm nature, they don't need a lot of attention or interactive play. They can certainly be playful, but are never demanding. Persians lend an air of tranquility to a home, and owners report they bring lots of joy too.

RAGDOLL

SIZE: medium to large	COAT: moderately long
COLOR: seal, blue, chocolate, lilac, red, and cream point colors, and a variety of patterns	
TEMPERAMENT: laid-back, friendly	

The Ragdoll is a fairly new breed that's become popular in recent years. It was developed in the early 1960s by a breeder who noticed that the kittens of her white long-haired cat, Josephine, had a lovely, laid-back disposition. Today's Ragdolls are all descended from Josephine, and the breed is known for its easygoing temperament. They are so relaxed that their name is a reference to their tendency to go limp when picked up. In the years since its inception, the Ragdoll has become a beloved staple in cat shows. In 2021, the breed was given the distinction of number one Top Cat by the Cat Fanciers' Association.

Ragdolls are large, with longish hair and long, fanciful plumed tails. Solidly built, the males weigh up to twenty pounds, while the females usually weigh ten to fifteen pounds. Their soft coats, despite being moderately long, don't need special attention—brushing once a week will suffice. Coat colors and patterns vary, but all Ragdolls have dazzling blue eyes.

In addition to their stunning good looks, the Ragdoll has a lovely personality. They seem to adore their humans; it's not unusual for this breed to run to the door to greet its owners when they get home. They are gentle and play well with kids and other pets. They enjoy playtime and are very receptive to being taught a few basic commands.

RUSSIAN BLUE

SIZE: medium	COAT: short
COLOR: silvery blue	TEMPERAMENT: reserved, gentle

The Russian Blue has an unmistakable look, with a lithe frame, lively green eyes, and a short, plush coat of solid silvery blue. They are known to be quiet but friendly. It may take a Russian Blue some time to warm up to new people, but you can expect them to cautiously come around in their own time. With familiar people, the Russian Blue is a devoted and affectionate friend.

The history of this breed is somewhat unclear. Some believe they are native to northern Russia and developed their thick coats to keep warm in the freezing temperatures. Others say they are the ancestors of the prized pet cats of Russian czars. No matter their origins, by 1875 they had made their first appearance at London's Crystal Palace Cat Show. And by the early 1900s, they were being imported to the United States. These days the Russian Blue is one of the most expensive cat breeds due to their relative rarity.

Russian Blues enjoy playing, but are never demanding. They also enjoy quieter activities, like relaxing next to their person or watching birds outside a window. They prefer a calm household and will shy away from too much loud activity. They don't mind spending some time alone, but will require your attention when they decide they want it. These elegant, low-maintenance kitties make great pets.

SCOTTISH FOLD

SIZE: medium	**COAT:** long or short

COLOR: a wide variety of colors and patterns, including white, chocolate, lilac, tortoiseshell, and tabby

TEMPERAMENT: sweet, adaptable

Scottish Folds are the only breed to have unusual ears that fold forward. Their chunky bodies and rounded heads give them the look of a teddy bear, and wide eyes give them an expression of pure sweetness. But it's not just their appearance that's so delightful; they have personalities to match. Friendly and adaptable, they are easy to travel with and don't mind meeting new people. With such a distinctive appearance and lovely temperament, the Scottish Fold has earned many fans.

The breed can be traced back to Scotland, when in 1961, a shepherd discovered a cat with folded ears on his neighbor's farm. Her name was Susie, and when she gave birth to a litter, the shepherd adopted one of the female kittens. He bred her with British Shorthairs, and the result was a cat with many of the same physical features as the British Shorthair, but with folded ears. Unfortunately, these cats were not always healthy; about a third of them would develop a skeletal disorder called osteodystrophy. It took breeders until 1978 to eliminate the gene that caused the defect. Now, the breed is regarded as healthy.

When Scottish Folds are born, they all have straight ears. It's not until they are three or four weeks old that their ears fold, although some cats' ears never do! It's not unusual for a Scottish Fold to be lacking the characteristic folded ear; these cats are not allowed to compete in cat shows, as they don't display the breed's standard, but are still used for breeding purposes. Although they are less desirable than their folded-ear brethren, they still make excellent pets!

SIAMESE

SIZE: medium	COAT: short
COLOR: seal point, chocolate point, blue point, lilac point	
TEMPERAMENT: gregarious, intelligent, vocal	

Siamese is one of the oldest breeds of pedigreed cats. They are elegant, with long, muscular bodies and long limbs and tails. Their almond-shaped eyes are a deep blue, and they have very large ears atop their wedge-shaped heads. Siamese are known for their colorpoint coats, with light coloration on their bodies and darker coloration on their extremities. Kittens are born white, and their colorpoints darken as they age.

Siamese cats of today are descended from the sacred temple cats of Thailand (then called the kingdom of Siam). As early as the 1350s, the breed was treasured by royalty and believed to have spiritual significance. The first Siamese made it to the United States in 1878, when one was given to President Rutherford B. Hayes as a gift from an American diplomat in Bangkok. A few years later in 1884, a pair of Siamese cats were brought from Bangkok to the United Kingdom, and from there the breed began to spread. In 1906, they were first recognized by the Cat Fanciers' Association.

Full of personality, this is not a breed for the faint of heart. Siamese are smart, active, and curious. They require a good deal of interaction and attention, and if they're not getting it, they'll find ways to entertain themselves, which may be less than favorable. They have an inquisitive nature and are extremely social. Siamese love their humans fiercely and want to be wherever they are. This is the perfect breed for someone looking to liven up their home—these chatty cats will talk your ear off. They are best suited to a place where they have continual human or animal companionship.

SNOWSHOE

SIZE: medium to large	**COAT:** short
COLOR: seal point or blue point, with white feet	
TEMPERAMENT: kind, playful	

The Snowshoe is a rare and fairly new cat breed. It originated in the late 1960s, when a Siamese breeder in Philadelphia was surprised to discover that a few of her Siamese kittens had unusual coloring—their feet were white as if they had just walked in snow. Excited by the potential to produce more cats with these distinctive markings, the breeder tried to re-create the cats' coloring by breeding her Siamese with American Shorthair. But she discovered that there was no foolproof way to create the coloring she wanted. Nonetheless, she and other breeders continued to experiment to create what we now know as the Snowshoe.

Not surprisingly, the Snowshoe has some characteristics in common with the Siamese. Like the Siamese, the Snowshoe is white at birth, with colorpoints that emerge with age. The Snowshoe also has blue eyes like the Siamese. Unlike the Siamese, however, they have a more rounded appearance. And, of course, Snowshoes have white fur on their feet like they're wearing socks.

The Snowshoe can best be described as charming. They love being around people and get along with other pets nicely. They want to be with their people and will move from room to room to make sure they're in on the action. They love to play but also enjoy relaxing on a lap. Like the Siamese, these can be chatty cats, but the Snowshoe's voice is softer and more pleasant. One thing this breed doesn't love is being left alone for long periods of time, so a house where someone (even another pet!) is home a lot is important.

SPHYNX

SIZE: medium

COAT: hairless except for fine hair on the nose, feet, and ears

COLOR: a variety of colors and patterns, including black, chocolate, lavender, tabby, tortoiseshell, and calico

TEMPERAMENT: outgoing, affectionate

Sphynx have a number of interesting physical features that set them apart from other breeds. Most notably, they have no hair. Their muscled, wrinkly bodies are almost fully bare, except for some slight peach fuzz (the amount varies from cat to cat). They also have extremely large, triangular ears that point skyward. Sphynx can have different coat colors despite not having hair—their skin, nose leather, and paw pads all have discernable color.

Sphynx require extra care and are not the right breed for someone who isn't prepared for a high-maintenance cat. Their paws must be cleaned regularly to dislodge the gunk that forms in their nail beds. They also have oily skin that requires special care; occasional baths are helpful but not often because you don't want to risk drying out their skin. Their oily skin also tends to leave stains on furniture, which creates more surfaces to clean. Sphynx owners must also be careful to keep their homes from getting too cold. Without fur, these cats can't keep themselves warm. Sphynx owners must also take care to keep their cats inside—exposure to the sun can cause sunburn, which can lead to skin cancer later.

For all the work involved in caring for a Sphynx, owners are handsomely rewarded. These cats are extremely affectionate and loving, eager to snuggle up with their favorite humans. They are also silly, smart, and friendly—there is never a dull moment with a Sphynx.